Amazing Beetles

EYEWITNESS JUNIORS

Amazing
Beetles

WRITTEN BY
JOHN STILL

Dorling Kindersley Education
London • New York • Stuttgart

A Dorling Kindersley Education Book

Project editor Louise Pritchard
Art editor Toni Rann
Senior editor Helen Parker
Senior art editor Jacquie Gulliver
Production Louise Barratt

Illustrations by John Davis, Jane Gedye
Photography by Jerry Young, Colin Keates
Animals supplied by Trevor Smith's Animal World,
Natural History Museum, London, Virginia Cheeseman
Editorial consultants The staff of the Natural History Museum, London
Special thanks to Carl Gombich and Kate Raworth for research

The publishers would like to thank the following agencies for their kind permission to reproduce the photographs:
Bruce Coleman Ltd/Freider Sauer pp. 12-13; Natural History Photographic Agency pp. 24-25

This is a Dorling Kindersley Education edition, 1994

Library of Congress Cataloging in Publication Data
Still, John.
Amazing beetles / written by John Still;
photographed by Jerry Young and Colin Keates
p. cm. - (Eyewitness juniors)
Includes index
Summary: Text and photographs introduce amazing members
of the beetle world, including scarabs and weevils.
1. Beetle–Juvenile literature. [1. Beetles.]
I. Young, Jerry; Keates, Colin, ill. II. Title. III. Series.
QL576.2.S75 1991 595.76–dc20 91–6516
ISBN 0-679-81519-8 (trade edition)
ISBN 0-7516-5054-4 (school edition)
ISBN 0-679-91519-2 (lib. bdg.)

Manufactured in Italy

Contents

What is a beetle?

Beetles are insects. Although they are small creatures, they are important. They clear away unwanted things such as dead plants and animals, pests, and even dung.

Head *Antenna*
Thorax
Back wing
Elytrum *Abdomen*

Protective case

A beetle's body is in three parts. Its front wings, or elytra (EL-ih-truh), are usually hard. They protect the soft upper parts of the beetle's body and the back wings if there are any.

Chafer grub

Chafer grub in pupal cell

Growing stages

All beetles lay eggs which hatch as larvae, or grubs. Larvae look more like worms than beetles. When they are fully grown, the grubs turn into pupae. Some kinds protect themselves inside a special case called a pupal cell. Finally the pupae turn into adults.

This chafer is shown much larger than life-size. It is really about 1 inch long.

Lift-off

Tiger beetles can just open their wings and fly. Other beetles must warm up in the sun first or climb to the tip of a leaf or stem for take-off.

The heavyweights

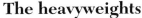

One of the biggest beetles is the goliath beetle from Africa. One measured 4½ inches. This is enormous compared to the smallest beetle, which is just ¹/₁₀₀₀ inch!

Elderly beetles

Most beetles live for a few weeks or months, but some can live for several years. Some kinds of darkling beetle may live for up to nine years.

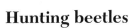

Hunting beetles

Some beetles eat plants, and others are meat eaters. Tiger beetles run fast on their long legs, hunting creatures such as flies and other insects for their supper.

Jaws

Beetles come in many different shapes, sizes, and colors. This beetle is a weevil. It has a long "snout," called a rostrum, with jaws at the tip. Female weevils use their rostrum to bore holes in which to lay their eggs.

Record numbers

This black and yellow beetle is a chafer. It is just one of over 350,000 kinds of beetle. In fact, there are more kinds of beetle than any other kind of animal.

Beetles everywhere

Many beetles are not seen often – they hide under stones, in wood, or in the soil. But if you looked hard you would find a beetle almost anywhere in the world – in water, on mountains, in caves, and even in deserts.

Island retreat
The Frigate Island beetle is found only on one tiny island in the Indian Ocean. It spends most of its time hiding under tree bark, where it feeds on rotting wood.

Rowing beetle
Whirligig beetles live on the surface of lakes and ponds. They are expert swimmers and use their middle and hind legs like oars to "row" across the surface. Their legs make sixty strokes per second.

Its white elytra hide this beetle on the white sand dunes where it lives

Beetle-longlegs
This darkling beetle of southwest Africa is only one of six kinds of beetle that has totally white elytra. Its body is just over 1 inch long and its legs are even longer.

Long legs keep the beetle's body well clear of the hot sand

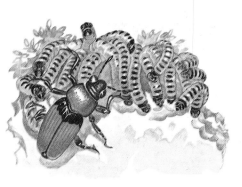

Fungus feast
Many beetles live on fungi, such as mushrooms, or on plants. This female beetle is showing her larvae the best places to eat.

Mobile home
Can you spot the beetles on this mouse? Several kinds of beetle are found in the fur of mice. Their real home is the mouse's nest, where they eat the larvae of other insects which live on the mice, such as fleas.

Household pest
Carpet beetles live in houses, and the larvae eat their way through carpets, curtains, and even clothes. One kind attacks insect collections and stuffed animals.

Breathing bubbles
The great diving beetle lives in ponds and can breathe underwater. It stores bubbles of air under its elytra, then absorbs the air through tiny holes in its body.

Leaf eaters

The leaf beetle family has some of the most colorful members in the world, and many of them have amazing habits.

Beetle variety
Leaf beetles live all over the world, and each kind looks different. Most are brightly colored, some have spines on their back, but some just look like a bump on a leaf.

Showing a leg
A jeweled frog beetle has strong back legs, but it does not use them for jumping. When in danger, the beetle raises these legs to scare the enemy.

A bloody nose
Bloody-nosed beetles get their odd name from the red liquid they squirt out when they are alarmed. The beetle looks as if its nose is bleeding.

Jumping beetles
Flea beetles use their back legs for jumping, just as fleas do. Flea beetles just 1 inch long can jump nearly 2 feet. That's like you being able to jump over about 15 cars!

This colorful tortoise beetle is about 1 inch long

Tight fit

This unusual-looking beetle is a tortoise beetle. Like most tortoise beetles, it lives in the tropics where it is hot all year round. It holds tight to a leaf with special "suckers," making it very hard for a hungry bird to remove it.

Under mother's wing

The females of some kinds of tortoise beetle gather their larvae under their wings when danger threatens. There is room for about twenty larvae to hide.

Wanted: dead or alive!

It is not just gangsters that are wanted by the police. The Colorado beetle is too. It eats potato plants, and one beetle can lay 2,500 eggs – enough to do a lot of damage when they hatch!

Arrow poison beetle

Various kinds of African leaf beetle are poisonous. The larvae eat poisonous leaves, making the larvae poisonous too. In southern Africa, Bushmen use the pupae to make poison arrows for hunting.

Meat eaters

There are many members of the animal kingdom that eat meat, and beetles are no exception. Some beetles prefer dead animals; other beetles are fierce hunters and killers.

Beetles in jackets

Rove beetles need to move fast to catch other insects. Many have a small, light wing case. They look as if they are wearing a jacket.

Beetle rover

This handsome rove beetle is about 1 inch long. It hunts for its food and is particularly good at snatching up insect larvae which are feeding on dead animals.

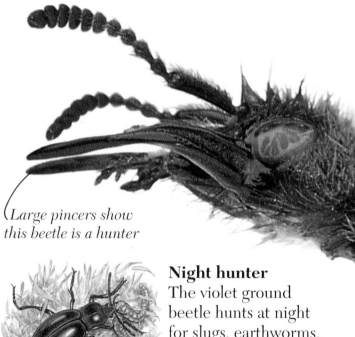

Large pincers show this beetle is a hunter

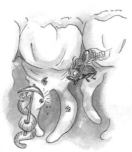

Night hunter

The violet ground beetle hunts at night for slugs, earthworms, and small insects. It chops them up with its sharp jaws.

Tooth beetles

People used to think that a toothache was caused by a little worm tunneling through the tooth. They would put a beetle in their mouth to eat the worm!

No laughing matter
Many beetles live in ants' nests. One kind of rove beetle begs food from the ants by tickling them with its antennae. Then it eats the ants' eggs and larvae too.

Grave diggers
Sexton beetles are very good at finding dead animals. They bury the animal by digging out the earth beneath it. Then the female lays her eggs underground, and when the larvae hatch, they have a meat feast!

Pond predator
The great diving beetle is a fierce hunter in ponds and lakes. Even small frogs and fishes are not safe.

This rove beetle raises its tail when it is about to attack

That's using your head!
The larvae of tiger beetles hunt almost as well as their parents do. The larvae of some kinds live in a tunnel in the ground and use their head as the door. They leap out and kill any insect unlucky enough to walk on their head.

Garden friends

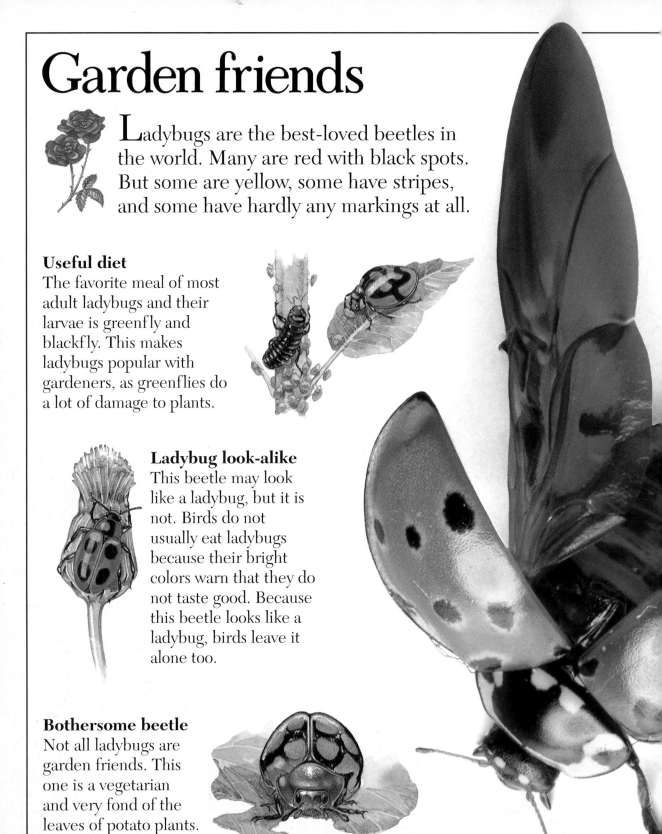

Ladybugs are the best-loved beetles in the world. Many are red with black spots. But some are yellow, some have stripes, and some have hardly any markings at all.

Useful diet

The favorite meal of most adult ladybugs and their larvae is greenfly and blackfly. This makes ladybugs popular with gardeners, as greenflies do a lot of damage to plants.

Ladybug look-alike

This beetle may look like a ladybug, but it is not. Birds do not usually eat ladybugs because their bright colors warn that they do not taste good. Because this beetle looks like a ladybug, birds leave it alone too.

Bothersome beetle

Not all ladybugs are garden friends. This one is a vegetarian and very fond of the leaves of potato plants.

Smell of danger

If you touch a ladybug it will probably let out a smelly yellow liquid from joints in its legs. Don't worry! It does this to put off its enemies.

Built for safety

Ladybugs have smooth, round bodies which are hard for a hungry ant or spider to attack.

Sleeping together

Adult ladybugs sleep, or hibernate, through the winter. They often crowd together under a piece of loose bark, on a post, or even in the house.

Count the spots

Some ladybugs are named after the number of their spots. These are 22-spotted ladybugs.

7-spotted ladybug – about ¼ inch long

Eyed ladybug – about ¼ inch long

Scarabs

The scarab beetle was so important to the ancient Egyptians that they carved and drew its shape on just about everything, especially their jewelry. There are more than 20,000 kinds of scarab beetle in the world, some of which have very strange tastes!

God-like beetles

The ancient Egyptians used the dung beetle as a symbol for their sun god. They believed that the sun was pushed around the sky in the same way the beetle rolls its ball of dung.

Smelly beetles

The best-known scarab beetles are the dung beetles. They collect animal dung and roll it into balls which they bury to lay their eggs in.

Not-so-tasty dinner

The female dung beetle shapes the dung into egg chambers underground. The larvae hatch in the dung, which becomes their first meal! After the pupa stage, they crawl up to the surface as adult beetles.

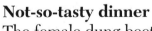

Like a rhino

Does this beetle remind you of a rhinoceros? The long horns on its head are the reason it is called a rhinoceros beetle. This male beetle is about 3½ inches long from the tip of its horn to the end of its body.

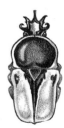

The strange horns may be used for displaying to a female or for lifting a rival out of the way

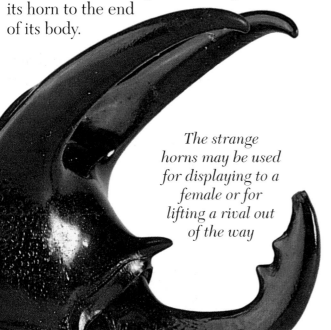

Many shapes and sizes

Some of the most amazing scarab beetles are the chafers. They come in many different colors, and the males have a variety of horns, hooks, prongs, or forks on their heads.

Big beetles

The Hercules beetle is a scarab beetle and one of the largest beetles in the world. Its horn can be up to 3 inches long – as long as its body!

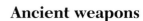

Ancient weapons

Some kinds of dung beetle cover their dung balls in clay before burying them. When these dung balls were first discovered they were mistaken for ancient cannonballs!

Long legs are needed for beetling along

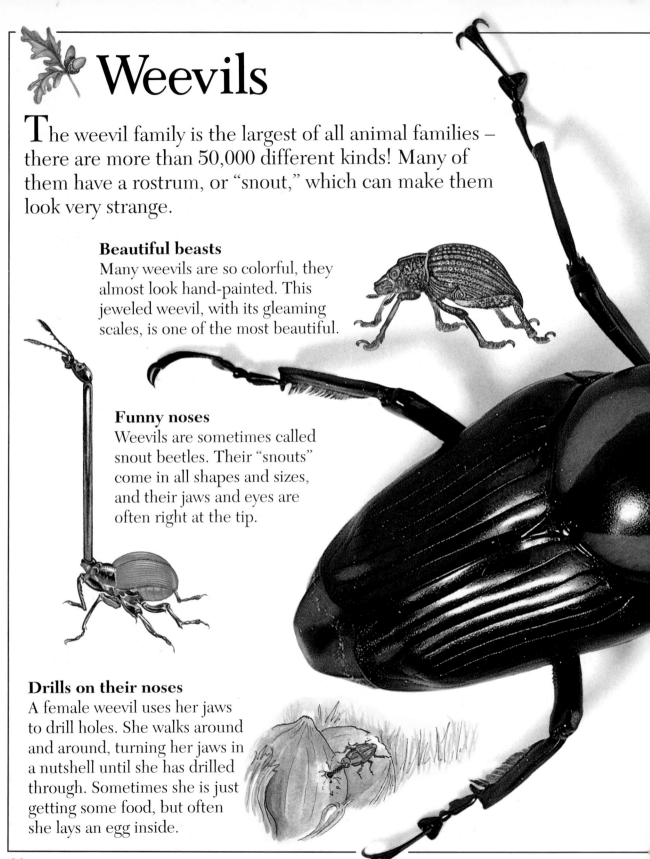

Weevils

The weevil family is the largest of all animal families – there are more than 50,000 different kinds! Many of them have a rostrum, or "snout," which can make them look very strange.

Beautiful beasts
Many weevils are so colorful, they almost look hand-painted. This jeweled weevil, with its gleaming scales, is one of the most beautiful.

Funny noses
Weevils are sometimes called snout beetles. Their "snouts" come in all shapes and sizes, and their jaws and eyes are often right at the tip.

Drills on their noses
A female weevil uses her jaws to drill holes. She walks around and around, turning her jaws in a nutshell until she has drilled through. Sometimes she is just getting some food, but often she lays an egg inside.

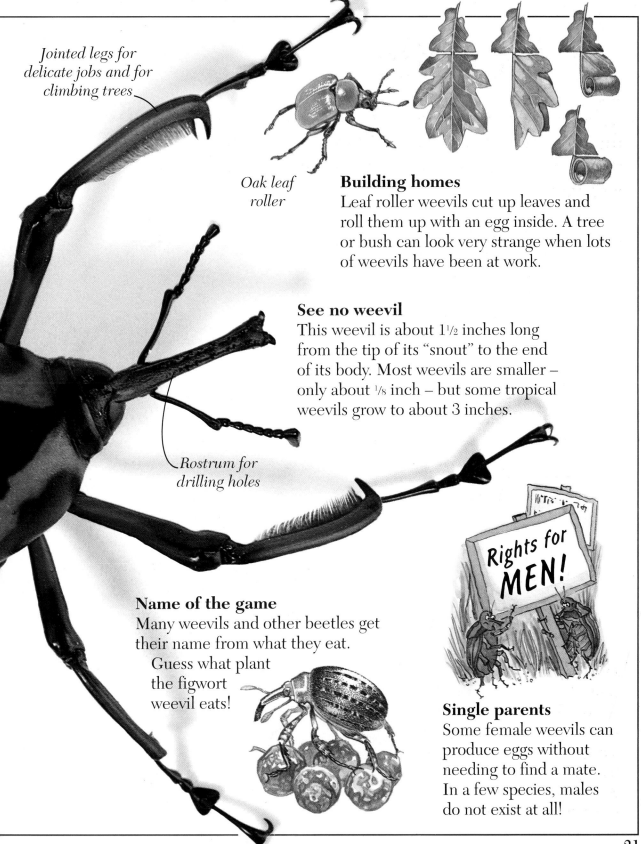

Jointed legs for delicate jobs and for climbing trees

Oak leaf roller

Rostrum for drilling holes

Building homes
Leaf roller weevils cut up leaves and roll them up with an egg inside. A tree or bush can look very strange when lots of weevils have been at work.

See no weevil
This weevil is about 1½ inches long from the tip of its "snout" to the end of its body. Most weevils are smaller – only about ⅛ inch – but some tropical weevils grow to about 3 inches.

Name of the game
Many weevils and other beetles get their name from what they eat. Guess what plant the figwort weevil eats!

Rights for MEN!

Single parents
Some female weevils can produce eggs without needing to find a mate. In a few species, males do not exist at all!

Flying colors

There are lots of beautiful beetles in the world. Some are brilliantly colored, others have amazing patterns. Many find their own design extremely useful.

Waspish
Many beetles look like other insects which have a sting or are poisonous, so that enemies will leave them alone. Wasp beetles are colored just like wasps, and they move like wasps too.

Color change
The bright pattern on this leaf beetle helps to disguise its shape on a flower. The colors are caused by liquids and can change as the beetle moves around.

Seed beetle
During the day, this seed look-alike allows itself to be blown around like a seed. At night, when there are fewer enemies around, it uses its legs to move!

Strong claws are useful for climbing

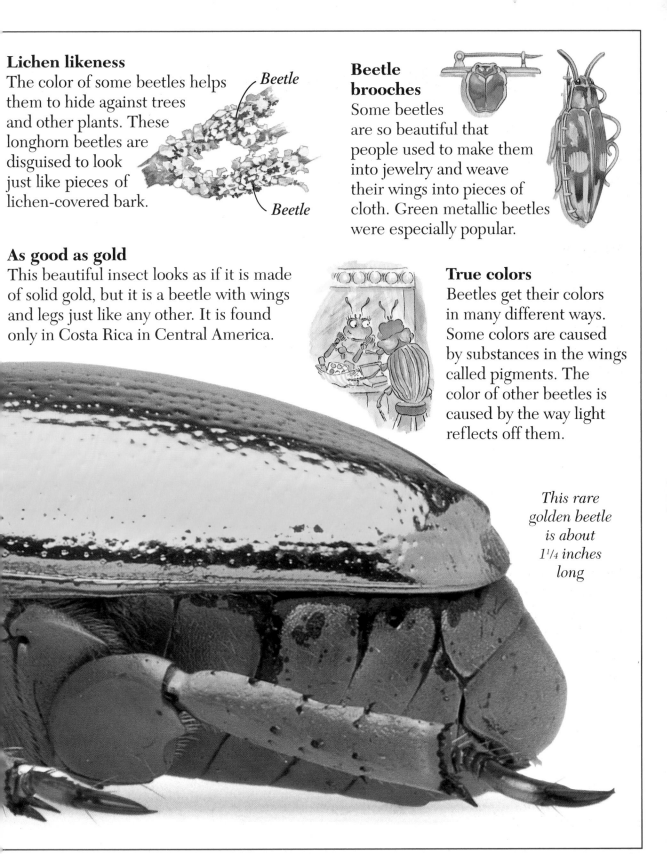

Lichen likeness

The color of some beetles helps them to hide against trees and other plants. These longhorn beetles are disguised to look just like pieces of lichen-covered bark.

Beetle

Beetle

As good as gold

This beautiful insect looks as if it is made of solid gold, but it is a beetle with wings and legs just like any other. It is found only in Costa Rica in Central America.

Beetle brooches

Some beetles are so beautiful that people used to make them into jewelry and weave their wings into pieces of cloth. Green metallic beetles were especially popular.

True colors

Beetles get their colors in many different ways. Some colors are caused by substances in the wings called pigments. The color of other beetles is caused by the way light reflects off them.

This rare golden beetle is about 1¼ inches long

23

Shock tactics

Beetles, like most other insects, make a delicious meal for many other animals. In order to survive, some kinds of beetle have developed amazing ways of escaping.

Click trick
If a predator picks up a click beetle it may get a surprise. The beetle arches its back, and a peg underneath clicks out of place with a "ping" in the predator's mouth. If the beetle is dropped on its back, it clicks again – hoping to land on its feet next time!

Smelly cocktail
Anything that dares to attack a devil's coachhorse may well change its mind. The beetle will lift its tail and make a terrible smell! It is also known as the cocktail beetle.

Rapid fire
When a bombardier beetle is attacked, it shoots! A mixture of hot chemicals explodes from its rear end, sometimes with a pop. Having shocked a predator into retreating, the beetle can hide. But if it has to, it can fire up to 500 times a second!

Jet-propelled
Camphor beetles can fire themselves across a pond by shooting out a gas. They can reach speeds of up to 2½ feet per second. That's 150 times their own body length per second.

Gap trap
The goliath beetle can move its head forward, leaving a gap at the top of its wing case. Hungry animals sometimes get caught when the beetle snaps shut – with painful results!

This beautiful blister beetle is about ¹/₂ inch long

Don't touch!
Blister beetles have very bright colors which act as a warning to leave them alone. Many of them give off a strong chemical, and your skin will blister if you touch them.

Ready, aim, fire!
When alarmed, many tropical ground beetles spray a nasty chemical. They take aim at their enemy and usually hit the target – in the eye!

Playing dead
Many beetles pretend to be dead when frightened. The Colorado beetle folds in its legs and antennae and lies on its back, completely still.

Winning ways

An important job in a beetle's life is to find a mate. Different beetles use different tactics for this, some of which are unusual.

Head-to-head combat
Longhorn beetles lay their eggs in tree stumps. The male claims a stump and guards it fiercely while he waits for a female. If another male comes along, the two males try to push each other off.

Beetle mania
Beetles of the same kind sometimes get together in one place to give themselves a good chance of finding a mate. Soldier beetles gather around flowers that they like.

Male stag beetles have much larger "antlers" than the females

Beetle lights
Glowworms and fireflies use a special organ in their body to flash a light and attract a mate. When thousands of one kind flash together in a tree, they can be seen for miles.

Side view of the stag beetle

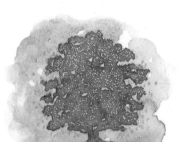

Including its fierce-looking jaws, this male stag beetle measures about 3 inches long

Knock on wood

The deathwatch beetle causes great damage to old buildings by tunneling into the wooden beams. To attract the attention of a mate in a different tunnel, it taps on the wood.

Trick of the light

Each kind of glowworm has its own flash code which a mate can recognize. But sometimes glowworms flash a different code to trick another beetle into coming closer – then they eat it!

Jaws for brawls

Male stag beetles have large jaws which they may use in wrestling matches with other males. But the jaws are not as strong as they look, and the beetles do not often hurt each other.

Smells good!

Some beetles attract a mate to their tree with their own perfume. Jewel beetles give off a special chemical that smells wonderful to a mate.

Friend or foe

Many beetles are useful to humans, others are pests, and it is often hard to tell which is which. Beetles which are foes as larvae can be friends as adults; some are a nuisance all their life.

Dinner invitation

Many beetles are welcome guests. One kind of beetle was brought to North America to stop gypsy moths from destroying trees. Each beetle could eat up to 400 gypsy moth caterpillars a year.

This red-spotted longhorn is about 2½ inches long – not including its antennae!

Elm bark beetle

Tree killers

Bark beetles tunnel in trees, making patterns under the bark. They don't mean to harm the trees, but sometimes they carry diseases. The elm bark beetle spreads Dutch elm disease.

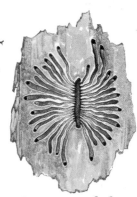

Pattern made by the elm bark beetle

Red-spotted longhorn beetle

Harmless adults

This longhorn beetle is easy to recognize by its long antennae. Adult longhorns do not cause much damage. But the larvae tunnel through all kinds of wood, often stopping a tree from getting enough of its own food.

Pest and pal

About 100 years ago, the boll weevil came to North America and ate the cotton plants from which the farmers made their money. The farmers began to grow other crops as well as cotton. They made more money by farming this way, and Enterprise, a town in Alabama, built this statue to thank the weevil!

Trouble underground

Wireworms are the larvae of click beetles. They crawl through the soil, annoying farmers and gardeners by eating the roots of plants.

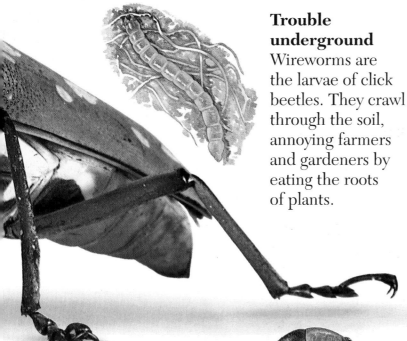

Greenhouse guests

Most ladybugs are definitely our friends. This kind of Australian ladybug is put into greenhouses on purpose to eat mealybugs.

Worm or beetle?

Woodworms are beetle larvae. They tunnel through dry wood like furniture and come out as adults. If you see small holes in your table, it is too late to catch the worm. The beetle has flown!

Index